# SEX EDU

# FOR

# 7 YEAR OLDS

## EMPOWERING PARENTS WITH THE

## RIGHT APPROACH

## TO SEX EDUCATION

ROBIE M. EMBERLY

Sex education for 7year olds

**Robie M. Emberly**

## TABLE OF CONTENTS

Sex education for 7year olds

## <u>CONCLUSION</u>

# INTRODUCTION

You have the capacity to be the most influential source of sexual education and advice for your children.

There is no better source of sex education than you! If you start talking about sex and sexuality with your children at an early age and follow the steps outlined here, your children will be in the best possible position to develop into sexually healthy and responsible teenagers and young adults

# CHAPTER ONE

## SEX EDUCATION FOR 7 YEAR OLDS

Parents frequently have a lot of questions about sex education.

Where do I begin?

So, what am I going to say?

When am I going to say it?

Since we were children, sex education has (happily) evolved. A huge one-time conversation isn't going to cut it when it comes to sex education (even if you think you have covered everything). It's all about having a lot of tiny, frequent, and repetitive talks with your child these days.

So, why do you feel the need to discuss all of this with your children?

To begin with, your children will learn about sex from their peers, from surfing the internet, and from watching television. By entering first, you ensure that they receive the correct information and, more significantly, that they are aware of your feelings on the subject.

Second, you're influencing what your children will do regarding sex in the future. Children who receive effective sex education are more likely to postpone having sex and, if they do, to avoid unplanned pregnancies and sexually transmitted illnesses.

**Here** is a list of the various aspects of sex that children should be aware of at some point in their lives. The themes and ages are provided as a suggestion only, and are based on what we currently know about child sexual development and how to keep our children healthy and safe in today's environment.

## TEACHING YOUR CHILD ABOUT LOVE AND RESPECT

To truly comprehend what true love is and to identify when you've found it, you'll need a certain level of emotional intelligence and developmental maturity. We don't spend a lot of time or effort teaching our kids how to identify love.

As a result, parents must devote a significant amount of time and energy to teaching their children about love and how to recognize it when it comes. There's a lot of intensity and a lot of emotions masquerading as love out there. Many individuals have experienced the feelings, emotions, and attitudes

Sex education for 7year olds

associated with love in a relationship only to find that they were insufficient to form an enduring bond.

That is, what we mistakenly thought was love turned out to be a sort of passion, infatuation, or desire.

Our children face substantially more difficulties in coping with the subject of love than many of us, and far more than our parents and grandparents.

Because they live in a culture where a higher proportion of teens and young people participate in sexual behavior, this is the case. When it comes to sex, things are a lot more complex when a relationship goes bad. As a result, today's young people's misidentification of love has considerably more catastrophic consequences than it did for many of us as children.

A youngster nowadays may assume she is in love and approach intimate sexual situations far more soon than prior generations.

## HARMFUL SEXUAL SIGNALS YOU MAY BE PASSING TO YOUR CHILD

However, you, the parent, must be addressed first and foremost. What type of sexual cues do you send to your child?

Sex education for 7year olds

How many of these have had a negative influence on your kid, contributing to their sense of apprehension and confusion?

Do you encourage your little boy to be courageous, tough, and strong?

Do you let your nine-year-old daughter wear low-cut shirts and short skirts, and do you let her use makeup? Do you want to be friends with your child but struggle with setting limits and saying no?

You need to be your child's first inspiration. What you do and how you do them matters the most. Re-examine your lifestyle.

# BABIES AND TODDLERS (0-24 MONTHS)

- Their body part names—yes, the penis and vulva as well!
- Allow them to grab their vulva or penis during bath time or nappy changes. And then explain why it is good or bad do so
- Begin by emphasizing the contrasts between guys and girls: boys have penises, while girls have virginas.

Sex education for 7year olds

- Begin by discussing the functions of our body parts: urine is expelled via the virgina, and feces are expelled through the anus (and it is okay to use appropriate slang, just not all of the time).
- Start teaching nudity boundaries if they enjoy being nude all the time — there is a time and a place to be naked (and it isn't in the park!).

**They're in need of assistance.**

At this age, sex education isn't technically possible. It's really just a matter of allowing your youngster to explore their entire body and beginning to point out simple gender differences. When labeling their body parts, include their penis or virgina and discuss what they can do - 'yep, that is your penis, and your wee (urine) comes out of there!' The ultimate goal is for your child to feel at ease with his or her entire body and to regard all parts as equal (with no shame).

**Infancy (2-5 years)**

**Our body.**

- The proper names of body parts, as well as their functions.

Sex education for 7year olds

- That boys and girls are both distinct and alike – Girls typically have a vulva and boys typically have a penis, but we all have nipples, bottoms, noses, hands, and other body parts.
- That our bodies are unique, and that it's alright to be unique.
- That our bodies can tell us what we're experiencing — we have a wide range of emotions that we can sense in our bodies.

## Privacy

- Some portions of the body are private and should not be exposed to the public eye.
- That there are private and public places and times - this might be a difficult concept for children to grasp because it is constantly changing. When your grandmother comes to visit, for example, it may be acceptable for your youngster to be naked at home, but not when the plumber comes!
- Respecting the privacy of others. They should knock and ask whether they can come in if the bathroom door is closed.

*Sex education for 7year olds*

- That they, too, have the right to privacy when using the restroom, bathing, or dressing.
- That discussions about bodies should take place in private at home and with their parents (not in the school yard).

## Touching ourselves

- It's fine to touch their penis or vulva, but there's a proper time and place for it.
- Set boundaries for genital play. Explain that while stroking one's own genitals might be pleasurable, it is a private action, similar to toileting, and should be done in a private location, such as their bedroom.
- If your child grabs their genitals while out socializing, gently remind them that their hands should not be in their trousers. Don't make a big deal about it while they're doing it since it makes them feel safer. They'll eventually grow out of it!
- Take a deep breath, politely interrupt them, urge them to get clothed, and divert them with another toy or activity if you find yourself playing 'doctor' with a friend (looking at each other's

Sex education for 7year olds

genitals). You can talk about privacy and touching guidelines later.

# HOW ARE BABIES MADE?

# THE RIGHT ANSWERS TO YOUR CHILDS QUESTION ABOUT CHILD BIRTH

- Trees drop seeds, dogs have pups, and humans have babies, and all living things reproduce. When you see examples of reproduction, gradually start pointing them out.
- The uterus, the baby bag, or even the tummy (you'll learn more about this later) is all places where a kid grows within a woman.
- A baby needs both a man and a woman.
- A man's cell (sperm) and a woman's cell (egg) are required to generate a baby. The first thing most children ask is, "Where do I come from?"
- That a woman's kid develops within her. Keep things simple — they're just interested in learning the fundamentals. The specifics will be revealed at a later time.

*Sex education for 7year olds*

- If they ask how the baby is born, simply tell them that it is born through the woman's stomach or vaginal canal.
- That having children is something grownups should do rather than something children should do. Make it a habit to remind them of this every time you bring it up. You could say "**You know mummy and daddy love you, and mummy and daddy are grownups, which is why they are able to have kids and take care of them**.

**Touching and body ownership**

- That people are in charge of their bodies and have the authority to determine who has access to them (you included).
- If someone doesn't want you to embrace or touch them, it's not okay (and vice versa).
- That there are instances when an adult, such as a doctor or nurse, has a legitimate reason to examine or touch their body.
- That we don't hide our bodies from each other. Surprises and gifts can be part of a secret.
- That they can always tell you about anything that bothers or amuses them.

Sex education for 7year olds

## The Support Your Child Needs

The easiest age to teach is preschoolers. They're like empty sponges, eager to absorb any and all information. If they haven't received an explanation that makes sense to them, they will concoct their own explanation. Prepare to repeat yourself because they forget easily and occasionally they don't understand or only hear part of what you say the first time. And don't forget to clarify what they're saying so you can offer them the correct answer!

You want to establish yourself as their go-to information source. This entails being open and honest when it comes to answering their queries concerning babies.

By responding, you're sending the message to your child that they may talk to you about anything and that you're a trustworthy source of knowledge. This is beneficial, especially once they begin to interact with other children.

# CHAPTER TWO

## MIDDLE CHILDHOOD

Many children are curious about how babies are formed around the age of five and may ask questions about it.

**'How did the baby get inside your uterus,'** your child might wonder. Inquire about your child's opinion. This enables you to comprehend what your youngster already understands. Then you can simply explain it, providing as much detail as you're comfortable with. For example, "a man's sperm and a woman's egg combine to produce a child."

It's also a good idea to explain that sexual intercourse is something adults do when they both want to, and that it's not something kids should do.

You could also mention that babies can come into households through other methods such as IVF, adoption, foster care, or grandparent care.

You do not need to wait until your child asks you questions. You should initiate a conversation when the need arise. "Have you ever wondered how you were born and where you came from?' might be an excellent approach to get a conversation started. If you come across a pregnant mother,

Sex education for 7year olds

tell your youngster, "That woman has a child developing inside her."

You may explain that when a man and a woman have sexual intercourse, the guy inserts his penis into the lady's vaginal canal. "Dad and mom married because they love one other, and you are proof of our love for each other, since you were formed with love... from daddy's sperm and mama's ovaries."

And what if your child asks you what a sperm is and what ovaries are?

Ovaries are eggs in mummy's uterus inside mummy's virgina and a sperm is like a fertilizer from daddy's penis that fertilizes the eggs and this should only happen when two grown up persons who are married and in love have sex.

Here are things your child should know at age 5-8

**Our Body**

- Know the terms for penis, testicles, scrotum, anus, vulva, labia, vagina, clitoris, uterus, and ovaries while discussing about male and female body parts.
- To have a basic understanding of the internal reproductive organs, including the uterus, ovary, fallopian tubes, urethra, bladder, and bowel.

Sex education for 7year olds

- That bodies are available in a variety of shapes, sizes, and colors.
- Both boys and girls have body regions that can be pleasurable to touch.
- To be able to care for their own body, including private areas, hair, teeth, skin, and other bodily functions.
- Having the ability to say(refusal skills ), "Stop, I don't like it."

## Puberty

- That as they grow older, their bodies will alter.
- Puberty is a period of physical and emotional transition.
- If they're curious about the changes, simply explain that this is the stage where they mature into adults.

## Sexual Intercourse

- That a baby can be conceived when a man's sperm combines with a woman's ovum, and that this normally occurs through sexual contact (IVF is another way).
- When sperm leave the man's penis and enter the woman's vagina, a baby is formed. They subsequently make their way to the egg's location. After then, the egg and the sperm combine to form a baby.

Sex education for 7year olds

- Adults have sex, and it is a natural, normal, and healthy part of life for them.
- Adults frequently kiss, hug, touch, and engage in other sexual behaviors with one another in order to show affection and make each other feel good.
- That sex is an adult activity that is not appropriate for children.'
- Adults have the option of having or not having a child.

**Sexual Behavior**

- All sexual activity, such as masturbation and sexual intercourse, is considered private.
- That it is not appropriate for children to look at photographs of naked individuals or people having sex on the internet. You should also talk to your youngster about what they should do when they come across such content anywhere (not IF they but WHEN they).
- Explain the distinctions between heterosexual, gay, and bisexual sexual orientations.

**Love**

Sex education for 7year olds

- Love entails feeling deeply and warmly for oneself and others.
- There are various sorts of love that people might experience.
- People show their love for their parents, relatives, and friends in a variety of ways.
- When two people are romantically connected to each other and spend their free time together, they are said to be dating.
- Dating begins in teenage.
- Throughout their lives, people might have a variety of romantic relationships.

## Friendships

- You can choose to have a large number of friends or a small number of pals.
- Various forms of friends are possible.
- Friends can be enraged at each other while yet remaining friends.
- Friends get to know one other by spending time together.
- Friendships can be hurtful to one another.
- Honesty is critical in friendships.
- Male or female, friends can be older or younger.

Sex education for 7year olds

## Families

- Families come in many different forms.
- Over time, families can alter.
- Every team member has a distinct contribution to make.
- Members of a family look out for one another.
- Families have norms in place to make it easier for them to coexist.
- A family can exist in multiple locations while yet remaining a family.

## Personal qualities

- Everyone, including children, has rights.
- People use a variety of methods to communicate.
- It is acceptable to seek assistance.
- Begin by practicing decision-making in your own house.
- All decisions have positive and negative repercussions.
- Make an effort to be aggressive.
- To overcome a problem or conflict, practice your negotiation abilities.

Sex education for 7year olds

## They Assistance Your Child Need

This is the moment when your children believe and absorb whatever you say, so take advantage of it to establish yourself as their primary source of information. They'll get it from somewhere else if you don't (friends and the media).

There's a tremendous difference between what a 5-year-old needs to know and what an 8-year-old needs to know; as they get older, you'll have to offer them more information and repeat yourself a lot more!

Try to be as honest and straightforward as possible when responding to their queries.

'What do you think?' is a good question to ask to figure out what they already know and what they want to know. Make sure you offer them enough information so they don't come to the wrong conclusion. For example, if you say a kid is born when a man and woman sleep together, they might interpret that to mean when they sleep close to each other. Check to see whether they've grasped what you've stated and if they have any additional questions.

Because some children do not ask questions, it is up to you to initiate the conversation. You can do this by seeking for opportunities to initiate a discussion on a daily basis.

Sex education for 7year olds

— a pregnant woman, a couple on TV kissing, menstrual products in the bathroom.

# CHAPTER THREE

## HOW TO BE YOUR CHILDS SEX TUTOR (12 AND ABOVE)

Some children are interested in sex topic, while others are not. Both are perfectly normal. Once adolescents reach puberty, they will begin to consider sex as something they might want to undertake in the future. By having a talk about sex with your child, you are letting them know that they can come to you with any questions they may have.

**What you should let them now...**

- Additional information on sexual intercourse and other sexual behaviors.
- Basic knowledge regarding STIs (Sexually Transmitted Infections) as they may have heard about them — infections can be transmitted during sexual activity, but there are techniques to make sex safer.
- Basic information on how to avoid being pregnant – there are steps you can take to avoid becoming pregnant.
- Sexual ideals and attitudes of their parents - love, dating, contraception, when it is OK to become sexually active, and so on.

Sex education for 7year olds

- When kids reach puberty, they will gradually become more sexual and develop romantic feelings for their friends.
- That same-sex fantasies and attraction are common once puberty begins and may not always reflect sexual orientation.
- In pornography, sexuality is exaggerated.
- How to be cybersmart and how to use their phones responsibly.
- Respectful partnerships have certain features.

## Puberty

- Girls must be aware of the importance of being prepared for their first menstruation.
- Ejaculation and wet dreams are important concepts for boys to understand.
- When girls begin to have periods and boys begin to produce sperm, this fertility occurs.
- That after puberty, both boys and girls are capable of having children.

## The Support Your Child Needs at This Age

This could be your last opportunity to speak with your child while he or she is still eager to listen! As they approach adolescence, they begin to rely more on their peers for knowledge and answers. This implies you should make it clear to them that they are welcome to come to you and discuss anything (and I mean anything).

So, be honest with them and provide them more information. If you don't know the answer to their query, team up with them to find it. Share your values and opinions about it, particularly when it comes to themes like love, dating, sexual intercourse, and contraception.

You'll need to get creative and come up with fresh ways to engage them in conversation (give them a book, talk to them while driving them somewhere, discuss something you both see on TV). You can also assist them in honing their decision-making, communication, and assertiveness abilities.

## Adolescence and Beyond

If you haven't started talking to your children about sex at this point, you should! It's never too late to begin, but it will be much more difficult!

Adolescence is the time when sex education becomes truly sexual! There are many difficult topics out there, like dating, contraception, when to have sex, and how to say "no," to mention a few.

Sex education for 7year olds

Talking to your children from a young age has the great advantage of arming them with the knowledge they need to make appropriate sex decisions. You'll also develop a relationship with them in which they feel comfortable talking to you about anything — and I mean anything!

The information you've provided your child is vital, but the fact that you're talking about it is much more so! That is what is most important!

# CHAPTER FOUR

## HOW TO FIND TEACHABLE MOMENTS FOR SEX EDUCATION

Teachable moments are regular occurrences that allow you to talk about sex with your child.

They allow parents to discuss specific sexuality issues with their children. Teachable moments can also help you and your children address sex in an open and continuing manner.

Teachable moments are a simple and straightforward method that any parent can master quickly. You only need to start looking for them and working with them for a few weeks, and you'll soon be having numerous conversations with your children about sexuality.

## THE THREE TEACHABLE MOMENTS

Three things are required for a teachable moment.

First and foremost, it necessitates an **open relationship** between you and your children — you must be willing to discuss sexuality with your children!

Second, you'll need a **catalyst**, which is an event or thing that emphasizes the sexual point, often known as an educational moment. A catalyst is the conversation starter, the reason why the teachable moment is taking place at that particular time and location.

Third, a teachable opportunity necessitates the knowledge of a **sexuality fact**. You can almost always discover a sexual meaning in anything since sexuality is such a big topic.

Keep in mind that sexuality entails more than just having sex. Discuss the other aspects with your child, such as affection, trust, respect, responsibility, and closeness.

## HOW TO FIND TEACHABLE MOMENTS

Catalysts, or the cause/trigger for a teachable moment, can be found in many areas. They can be found in the following places:

**Each day's routine**

- when changing a nappy, talking about the parts of the body
- When it comes to bathing the kids, there is a lot of concern about inappropriate touch.

Sex education for 7year olds

- 'Mum, Tim claimed I was gay today,' for example, telling about what happened throughout their school day and what it implies.

## When you're out shopping or driving

- upon witnessing a pregnant woman, talking about how a baby grows inside its mother
- when you see two men holding hands in the park, start chatting about homosexuality.
- When you see a billboard with a model who is stereotypically skinny and attractive, you start talking about body image.

## Books, television shows/cartoons, movies, and music

- Referring to the fact that, contrary to popular belief, girls do sometimes fall in love with other girls rather than boys.
- discussing the meanings of a song's lyrics
- Selecting a book to introduce a topic, such as kissing/hugs to introduce touch boundaries.

## Historic Events

- discussing the media's most recent sex scandal

Sex education for 7year olds

- discussing occurrences at school, such as the first girl in the class to begin her period (menstruation)
- Special occasions, such as Child Protection Week and World Aids Day, should be discussed.

Basically, teachable moments may be found in almost every situation! You'll be shocked how many you find once you get started looking!

## TIPS ON UTILIZING TEACHABLE MOMENTS

When you have a cause to speak, it can be easier to identify an instructive opportunity.

For example, you may have heard on the radio about the huge number of children who come across pornography by accident.

So you decide to look for a teachable time to bring up the subject of pornography.

You will find it easier to identify the opportunity for the topic if you know what you want to talk about.

It could be as simple as noting that your youngster is watching YouTube videos.

Sex education for 7year olds

You may inquire as to what they're looking at and then casually suggest that they can occasionally find private movies or photos on YouTube.

It might be a simple comment or a 5-minute casual conversation.

### Tips for maximizing Teachable Moments

- To find out what your youngster thinks or feels, ask a gentle question.

'Look at that individual over there; why do you believe they have such a large stomach?'

'How do you feel about the fact that females always seem to fall in love with boys?'

'How do you feel about the fact that females always seem to fall in love with boys?'

**Give accurate information**

- 'That individual is carrying a child.'
- 'Yes, the majority of girls fall in love with boys, but they also fall in love with other girls.'

**Please share your own ideas**

Sex education for 7year olds

- 'Do you have any idea how that lady gave birth to that child?' To make it, I believe they required a unique male role.'
- 'Some people believe that falling in love with someone of the same gender is inappropriate. 'What are your thoughts on the subject?'

# CHAPTER FIVE

## HOW TO PROTECT YOUR CHILD FROM INTERNET DANGERS (PORN)

Knowing how to protect children from internet risks such as online pornography is one of the most difficult difficulties that parents face today.

Pornography was hard to come by when we were youngsters, and it mostly consisted of magazines stashed in your father's closet and illegal DVDs seen when no one else was around.

For today's youth, it's a different story, as it's now more difficult to avoid porn than it is to locate it. Parents must also learn how to protect their children from Internet threats such as online pornography.

Pornography is more accepted, accessible, and openly available than it has ever been.

With a single click of the mouse, children can read sexually explicit material ranging from soft-core (such as those found in Playboy) to hard-core (such as those available on the internet) (material depicting graphic sex acts, live sex show, orgies, bestiality, and violence). It's not simple to broach the subject of pornography with children.

*Sex education for 7year olds*

Most parents believe they are ignorant about the subject and are unaware of how 'nasty' and harmful modern-day porn is. It is our job to protect our children to the best of our abilities as parents.

However, how can we protect youngsters from online risks such as pornography?

Are children at risk from online risks such as porn?

Pornography isn't new, but the sheer volume of it and the ease with which we can obtain it are! The potential of exposure is substantially higher now that kids are spending more time online than ever before.

The type of pornography being seen has evolved, with significant degrees of violence directed towards women who look to be having a good time!

Porn sends the wrong messages to kids about what sex is all about, according to some study, and it can lead to dysfunctional sexual behavior as well as unfavorable attitudes toward women. It has the potential to be addicting and has a negative impact on a child's emotional and mental well-being.

As a result, it is more necessary than ever for parents to learn how to protect their children from the hazards of the internet.

**My Child Would Never Look at Porn!**
Sex education for 7year olds

Pornography is an internet hazard that no youngster is immune to, with children discovering it either by accident or via a desire to learn more about sex. The average age of first exposure to pornography is 11 years old, while some sources claim it can be as young as five years old.

There's a good probability your youngster will come across pornography as soon as they can use a search engine or view videos on YouTube. Even if you live in a technology-free home, your youngster may come across porn while outside.

You should have this chat with them regardless of their age.

## How Then Do I Protect My Children?

You may not be able to prevent your child from coming across internet threats such as porn, but you may reduce the potential harm by preparing them. No, talking about porn does not rob your child of his or her innocence. When they are caught off guard, this is what will happen!

**Here are a few ideas for parents!**

**Children should be warned.**

Warn your child that they may come across private photos or videos of adults doing intimate activities together, some of which may be naked and appear to be hurting each other. It's known as porn or pornography.

Sex education for 7year olds

## Where bad images can be found?

Tell your child that these images or videos may appear by accident on the web, tablets, cartoons, video games, YouTube, phones, and even books or magazines.

## What should children do if they come across bad photos

If they come across these images, they should immediately switch it off or turn away and speak with a parent or trusted adult. Assure them that they will not get themselves into any trouble.

## The rules of the family

Talk about your family's rules for using technology, such as computers, tablets, and other gadgets, such as time limits and public chat rooms.

The computer should be kept in the main living space, with the screen placed where it can be seen readily. Bedrooms should also be free of electronic devices.

## Filters for parental control

If your children are younger, you may wish to use software filters, child-friendly apps (such as YouTube Kids), or popup blockers. However, keep in mind that your youngster may encounter images in other ways, such as through peers or unfiltered computers.

**Continue the conversation.**

When it comes to teaching children, it takes a lot of dialogues. Have short, frequent conversations with your child in clear, direct, and age-appropriate language.

# THE TWO BIG WAYS TO TALK ABOUT SEX

When it comes to discussing difficult things with our children, such as children and pornography, there are two approaches we might take.

**Respond to their inquiries.**

First, we can respond to any inquiries that our children may pose. Fortunately for us, children are naturally curious about the world around them and will frequently inquire about things they don't understand or are interested in. aIf you're afraid about not knowing how to respond to their queries, I will leave some frequently asked questions and answers you could use in this chapter. It offers age-appropriate responses to the most common sex-related inquiries that children ask their parents.

**Use Books**

Sex education for 7year olds

The second step is for us to initiate the discussion. Because not all of us have children who inquire about sexuality, it is up to us, the parents, to find a way to bring the matter up on our own.

The difficulty then becomes how to bring up the topic of children and pornography without it feeling like a lecture (I don't know about your kids, but mine will immediately stop listening if they believe they're about to get a lecture). That means we'll have to come up with a strategy to start the discussion ourselves.

One approach that naturally and casually works for me is to begin a discussion using books.

So, how can we use a book or a story to start a conversation about children and porn? You may, for example, read a book to your children about a specific topic while conversing about it.

For example, I could wish to discuss pornography with my daughter. You have a couple of options for having the talk.

'Hey, I was looking through this book today and saw that it had a section on pornography in it,' you may say. Have you looked on the internet for something like that?'

Sex education for 7year olds

"Hey, remember that book we read last week about how you could find stuff on the internet that you didn't expect to find?" or anything along those lines?" So, I'm curious if you have seen anything that is not normal.'

If your child asks, "**What is pornography**?"

You could respond starting with a question, "What is pornography?"

Do you remember that book we read about finding things you wouldn't expect to find on the internet?

Well, pornography is one of them.

# CHAPTER SIX

## A SIMPLE APPROACH TO ANWERING YOUR CHILDS SEX RELATED QUESTIONS

It will only be a matter of time until your children inquire about the birds and bees. It all begins so simply "At the bus stop, mummy, someone told me how babies are made." *Gulp* I'm sure you're familiar with the scenario.

Today's children learn a great deal about sex via their peers and the internet. There's a lot of misinformation out there, and there aren't many safe settings for kids to raise questions, let alone have a great, helpful conversation.

However, "the chat," as scary or exhilarating as it may be, is not a one-time event. It could be the first of many opportunities to help your child develop into a sexual citizen who is responsible, polite, and powerful. The first step in this journey? Listen to them – throw aside all of your awkward feelings, whether you're feeling them or not, and really listen.

Paying attention to what your child says and addressing their sex/gender/relationship questions when they ask them is a great method to figure out what to tell them. You might also inquire as to whether or not the child has overheard their

*Sex education for 7year olds*

peers discussing something, so you can correct any inaccuracies in your response."

However, with so much information available, it can be difficult to give your children what they need to know in an age-appropriate manner. Respond to the child's interest and need to grasp what they hear, rather than looking for certain things to address at each age.

Don't teach the kid all you know about a subject; keep it basic and allow them to ask for more information if they require it.

Some caregivers won't be able to responsibly discuss sex with their kids. In a custody dispute, for example, being 'too open' could be a problem.

Rather than being the type of parent who won't answer any questions (or in great detail), tell the youngster that they asked a good question and that it's not an issue that they are curious. That way, at least a little sex-positivity can be inserted. It is never ethical to shame or chastise a youngster for having a sexual interest.

## THESE ARE SOME OF THE MOST RECENTLY ASKED QUESTIONS. KIDS INQUIRE OF THEIR PARENTS

Sex education for 7year olds

**Where do babies come from?**

"It's always vital to be ready to respond calmly and honestly, depending on the age, maturity, and readiness of the child who is asking this question."

"Babies are born from a mother's womb. You could tell a much younger child... but a child who is older, you can say something like "Babies come from mommy's uterus."

As a mother, you should hopefully promote body confidence in your child at an early age.

Teaching your daughter/son about her/his body and using the correct terminology when discussing puberty-related changes makes these types of queries easier to handle as they grow older."

**Can teenagers have children?**

"Yes, teenagers can have children. A girl can conceive if a sperm meets her ovary.

**TIPS**: For an easier approach, you can explain sex using trees and plants... seeds and roots...etc

You can leave it at that or add your family's values and beliefs to having sex at this age, keeping a baby at this age, and so on, depending on what the child wants to know, age

Sex education for 7year olds

appropriateness, and parent agreement if the child is being raised by more than one parent."

**How can people who aren't married have children?**

"As usual, (and this depends on age and if that child already knows the foundations of sex and sexual activities and does not need to be taught what sexual intercourse is), what I would say is:

"People have babies in a variety of ways. Isn't it wonderful to learn about how someone came into the world and into a family? Some couples have children by having sex with each other. The two adults are occasionally married, but they are also sometimes not married but in love or in a relationship. When someone becomes pregnant despite not intending to have a child, they are overjoyed to become a parent.

"Sometimes a couple or a single individual decides they want to create a family and seeks the help of a doctor who helps them conceive a child in a fertility clinic.

A person may also have a baby because they want to adopt a child. When a biological mother and father decide that it is best for someone else to raise their child, a person or couple agrees to raise the child in their household.'

**Do all girls have vaginas and all boys penises?**
Sex education for 7year olds

"No! The majority does, however regardless of the anatomy between your legs; you can feel like a guy or a girl (or neither!) Gender identity refers to how you feel about this, and it's crucial since it influences how you feel of yourself and how you want others to treat you.

**Must one be married before they have sex?**

"No, adults indulge in sex in a different of adult relationships for a number of reasons.

If two adults love each other and want to have sex but not marry, they can, and they are commonly referred to as "lovers" or "partners."

Always make sure to emphasize on Grown Ups and Adults as this helps to set the boundary on what kids should do and what adults/grownups are only allowed to do.

**How do people have sex?**

"Individuals of both genders may do similar things when they have sex because sex in partnerships is a method for people to care about each other and make each other happy." Kissing, cuddling, caressing, stroking, licking, and playing with sex toys are all activities that anybody may participate in.

**What are condoms?**

Sex education for 7year olds

"Condoms are a type of birth control that also protects against sexually transmitted infections. During sexual activity, they act as a barrier between the penis/vulva/mouth/anus, and so on.

Female condoms, also known as internal condoms. To avoid the transmission of STIs, sexual health specialists, including myself, strongly advise the use of condoms during every sexual activity for two grown adults who are capable of taking care of themselves."

## General Tips on Talking About Sex with Kids

Because there's no way to answer all of your child's inquiries, consider the following suggestions:

- Answers should be succinct and to the point.
- Make sure you're responding to the child's question.
- Determine what the youngster already knows or is considering.
- Answer honestly, but don't feel obligated to disclose the complete truth if it isn't acceptable for your age group.
- Allow the youngster to decide whether or not he or she requires any additional information beyond the original query.

Sex education for 7year olds

- After you've answered their questions, ask if they have any more.
- You don't have to answer everything at once or properly. After regrouping and investigating, you can always go back and reread it at your leisure.
- (Optional) Inquire if they learned about the issue or topic via a friend, another child, family member, the television, or the internet. Thank them for inquiring about it.

  You can say something like this- "Oh Johnny, that's a great question you just asked, and mummy is proud of you...but she wants to know if you heard it from your pals or from the television."

## INCLUDING YOUR MORAL VALUES

When talking to your child about sex and sexuality, it's vital to include your own ideas and values. When talking to your child about birds and bees, the first thing you should do is incorporate your own principles and ideas.

If you approach things this manner, you can be sure that your child will have a better understanding of the issue. You must remember that parents play a significant role in their children's lives, which is why you must influence them with

Sex education for 7year olds

good acts to guarantee that they make the best life decisions possible.

Here you will discover and comprehend some of the most effective and beneficial methods for discussing birds and bees with your child.

If you follow these guidelines, you'll be able to easily explain and discuss the actual world of sex with your child.

## Discussing Sex in an Effective and Useful Way

Make sure you have adequate references to start your conversation with your child, as well as your own ideals and values. When it comes to sex situations and sexual issues, a parent with strong morals and values can be a huge help to their child.

## Defeat Embarrassment

It's normal if words like penis and vagina give you the creeps. You should practice saying these terms in private until you feel at ease discussing them with your child in a calm setting. If you do this, you will feel more at ease and calm while discussing sex with your child. This is considered one of the most effective strategies for fast reducing humiliation.

Make time to have open and ongoing conversations with your child.

According to research, teaching your child about sex and sexuality, especially while they are young, is really important. It is, nevertheless, vital that you continue to educate children on this issue as they get older.

It's a fact that your child will have to deal with sex life and sexuality for the rest of their lives, and it's hard to cover all of the important subjects in one conversation.

If you've finally created open dialogue and discussion with your child, it'll be simple for you to use teachable occasions to continue educating your child about sex.

In addition, educational moments are commonplace. When you and your kid, for instance, see a pregnant lady or hear on the news about sexual assaults.

These enlightening moments can often devolve into sex-related debates. As a consequence, instructive moments can help you facilitate sex communication, especially as your child becomes older.

**Give your youngster specific and proven information.**

Sex education for 7year olds

One of the finest morals and values a parent can have is knowing sex facts and acquiring correct knowledge and data regarding sex circumstances.

In the last year, just surfing the internet offered access to extensive sex data. You might also get your child some age-appropriate books.

Tell your child that if you don't know the solution to a question, you'll research it and come back to them.

## Recognize the Stage of Development

Telling your youngster about nocturnal emissions and menstruation after they've gone through it for a few months isn't helpful. The first thing you should discuss with your child before they reach puberty is sexual experiences and phases.

As a consequence, you'll notice that your child is less interested with what's going on with their body.

## Please don't lecture

Lectures should be avoided since most teenagers nowadays do not want to be told anything. The best thing you can do is supply enough details and facts, as well as engage in a full conversation about the topic.

*Sex education for 7year olds*

Although your kid is free to make their own sexual decisions, it is vital that you, as a parent, give them with the resources and knowledge they need to make well-informed judgments.

Instead of lectures, your child will benefit from conversations and debates. You may also rely on your child to pay attention to you and what you say.

**Teach children about the dangers and joys of sex.**

According to science, sex is not a bad aspect of life, and you have no need to be terrified of it. Some people, however, consider sex to be a potentially detrimental activity. In real life, sex is natural and beautiful, which is one of the reasons why your child should be well-versed in it.

They have a right to know about sexuality and sex, as well as how to deal with these issues in their lives. Discussing relationships and intimacy with your child will go a long way toward helping them understand the notion.

You should contact them as soon as possible as a parent to ensure that your child understands the issue of sex.

# CONCLUSION

You can see how our children will be in a good place by the time they reach puberty if you put what we've spoken about so far into practice. This is because they will regard us as accessible; they will have thought about sexual cravings and how to control them; and they will have thought about the value of love, respect, and trust in a relationship. As our children advance through middle school and into high school, our effect on the sorts of sexual activities they engage in and don't engage in should become increasingly apparent.

Printed in Great Britain
by Amazon

27246303R00036